WHEN FAITH CRUMBLES

HARD EVIDENCE FOR ROCK-SOLID FAITH

MARK FINLEY
with STEVE MOSLEY

Pacific Press Publishing Association
Boise, Idaho
Oshawa, Ontario, Canada

Edited by B. Russell Holt
Cover design by Center Graphics Adventist Media Center
Typeset in 10/12 New Century Schoolbook

Copyright © 1993 by
Pacific Press Publishing Association
Printed in the United States of America
All Rights Reserved

Unless otherwise noted, all Scripture quotations are taken from the New International Version.

Library of Congress Cataloging-in-Publication Data

Finley, Mark, 1945-
  When faith crumbles: hard evidence for rock-solid faith/ Mark Finley with Steven Mosley.
      p.   cm.
  ISBN 0-8163-1160-9
  1. Apologetics—20th century. I. Mosley, Steven R., 1952- II. Title.
  BT1102. F45 1993
  239—dc20   93-3818
                                                         CIP

96 97 ● 5 4 3 2

Contents

Introduction 5

Buried Evidence 7

A Life Written Beforehand 16

If God Is So Good 24

Why Millions Are Not Christians 32

A Tale of Two Tombs 40

Into the Inferno 48

The World of Tomorrow 56

Introduction

The evidence is accumulating. The facts are in. Recent archaeological discoveries have confirmed what we believed to be true all the time—the Bible is reliable. Throughout the centuries, there has been no significant tampering with or changing of the text. As recent news coverage has reported, ongoing examination of the Dead Sea Scrolls, discovered in 1947, confirms that God has faithfully preserved His Word down through the centuries.

Not only have the Dead Sea Scrolls confirmed the accuracy and authenticity of the text of God's Word, but archaeologists throughout the Middle East are continuing to unearth finds that testify to the truthfulness of the Bible. These amazing discoveries answer questions of thinking people everywhere. This is one of the reasons why thousands of former skeptics are now turning to the Bible.

In this little volume we shall explore the evidence for faith. I have complete confidence that you are honest in heart—that your desire really is to know truth. That is why you are reading this book. You may have a number of serious questions. You may wonder,

"How can I be certain the Bible is true?"

"Is Jesus really divine, or was He merely a good man?"

"If God is so good, why is the world so bad? Why is there

so much sickness and suffering and death?"

"How can a loving God torment millions in hell for thousands of years?"

"Why did Jesus have to die?"

These fundamental questions of Christianity find specific answers in archaeology, prophecy, history, and the Word of God. In this volume we will provide believable answers for inquiring minds. God has not erased all reasons for doubt. But He has provided sufficient evidence for faith. As you read these pages with an open mind, you will discover the reasonableness of Christianity. My research associate, Steve Mosley, and I are deeply impressed that this volume can make a significant difference. You can believe. And this belief will powerfully influence your whole life.

Our prayer is that the Holy Spirit will impress your heart with the accuracy of the Bible. That you will feel yourself drawn by the marvelous love of God, and that you will find rock-solid evidence for your faith.

Mark Finley

Buried Evidence

After three decades of waiting, the complete Dead Sea Scrolls are coming to life. A wide variety of scholars are finally getting access to them. But with this new publicity, we're hearing a wild assortment of sensational claims. Among them: Chinese symbols found on the margins of the Isaiah scroll point to the Messiah; a letter from Samson to Delilah has been found among the scrolls; Jesus was not born in Bethlehem, but in the Qumran community; He didn't die on the cross, but was given an anesthetic in His wounds, was later revived, and spent the rest of His days in a monastery.

With all these claims being tossed about in newspaper headlines, we're left wondering—just what do these latest Dead Sea Scroll discoveries reveal?

It was called "the academic scandal of the twentieth century." Four decades after the discovery of the Dead Sea Scrolls in the caves at Qumran twenty-five miles east of Jerusalem, about a fourth of the documents *still* had not been published. Scholars from all over the world were dying to study them. But the task of putting together the scroll fragments and deciphering them had been assigned exclusively to a close-knit team of eight scholars.

Everyone wondered what was taking them so long. Were

8 WHEN FAITH CRUMBLES

they hiding some new discovery that might threaten the faith? Were they just protecting their scholarly turf?

In September 1991, matters came to a crisis in Cincinnati. A group of scholars announced they had established the text for an unpublished Qumran document on their own. How? By using a concordance of the scroll materials and a sophisticated computer program, they identified overlapping material and somehow spliced it all together.

Shortly after the Cincinnati announcement, Huntington Library officials, custodians of a photographic set of the complete scroll collection, said they would open their vaults and grant all qualified scholars access to the scroll photographs! Researchers embarked on a "feeding frenzy." Scores of scholars couldn't resist the temptation to imagine sensational discoveries in what they were reading. So how have their claims held up?

Well, the supposed Chinese symbols on the Isaiah scroll haven't really stood the test. There was, apparently, a little too much scholarly imagination. And Samson's letter to Delilah must have been returned to sender; we have no real trace of it in the documents. The idea that Jesus was born in Qumran and was revived after His crucifixion proved to be a rehash of some very old speculation. No textual evidence supported it.

What, then, *does* this latest study of the scrolls prove? Nothing at all? Let me give you a few glimpses of what is very much an ongoing process of discovery.

First, the scrolls fill out the picture of Jewish life just before and during the time of Christ. They give us some insights into the turbulent times that gave birth to Christianity.

For some time, scholars have believed that the Dead Sea Scrolls were the product of a community of Essenes, an ascetic Jewish sect. Some scholars began to see this group as a forerunner of the Christian church. Like Christians,

BURIED EVIDENCE 9

the Essenes practiced baptism, and there seem to be certain common patterns of thought between the two groups. So were Christ's followers actually an Essene sect originally?

Well, as more and more scrolls come to light, increasing contrasts appear between New Testament teaching and the religion of the Dead Sea Scrolls. For example, the Essenes emphasized the law of Moses very strongly; early Christians presented the gospel of Christ as superseding the old ceremonial law. Some scholars now affirm that the scrolls help show how distinctive Jesus' message really was.

But the links we *do* find between the Dead Sea Scrolls and Christ are tantalizing. Here's a sentence from a Qumran fragment just recently published. It was written in Aramaic, several decades before the Gospels. "By his name shall he be hailed [as] the Son of God, and they shall call him Son of the Most High." This certainly sounds like a messianic prophecy, doesn't it? In fact, it almost parallels the annunciation recorded in the Gospel of Luke, in which the angel tells Mary that she will bear a child called "Son of the Most High" and "Son of God" (Luke 1:32, 35).

Much more scholarly work remains to be done, of course, but isn't it remarkable that the latest Dead Sea Scroll fragments are already giving us what appear to be glimpses of Jesus Christ? I can't help feeling that Jesus, as the fulfillment of the whole Old Testament system, will stand out ever more clearly as we understand more and more about the scrolls.

It seems to me that the discovery of the Dead Sea Scrolls has been a wonderfully providential event—occurring in this skeptical, secular twentieth century. You may have heard the story of how a shepherd boy stumbled on the scrolls, but you may not realize that this priceless find almost became shoe leather!

The year was 1947. Fifteen-year-old Mohammed ad

10   WHEN FAITH CRUMBLES

Dhib was looking for a lost goat when he idly tossed a stone into a cave on the side of the cliff. He heard the sound of crashing pottery. In that moment he could think only of evil spirits, and he rushed away.

By next morning he'd calmed down. In fact, he must have had a little bit of the "Indiana Jones" spirit in him; he persuaded a friend to return to the cave with him—there might be a treasure of gold inside! Imagine their disappointment when they found only broken pottery and some old leather scrolls. They didn't know what to make of their find, but they took one of the scrolls back to camp and unrolled it. It reached from one side of the tent to the other.

Later they went back for more. For weeks they wandered around with the scrolls, wondering what to do with them. Finally, they took them to Bethlehem, to Kando, a Syrian Christian who ran a grocery and cobbler's shop. Kando wasn't interested in the artifacts as scrolls, but he kept them. He thought the old material might be useful for mending shoes! The very thought that the oldest existing manuscript of the Bible might have been used for repairing shoes is still enough to make any scholar's heart stop beating! Can you imagine such a catastrophe?

At this point we pick up the exciting story with Elazar L. Sukenik, professor of archaeology at Hebrew University in Jerusalem. On Sunday, November 23, 1947, he received an urgent message from a friend, an Armenian dealer in antiquities. His friend said he had something of interest to show Sukenik but couldn't tell him what it was over the telephone. You may recall that during this period, British security forces had divided Jerusalem into military zones marked off with barbed wire barriers and guarded by sentries. The next morning, the friends met at the gateway to Military Zone B in Jerusalem; their historic conversation took place with barbed wire between them. From his briefcase, Sukenik's Armenian friend took a scrap of leather. On it was some Hebrew script. He said an Arab antiquities dealer from Bethlehem had come to him the day before with a tale of Bedouin boys who had brought scrolls that they claimed to have found in a cave. The boys had offered to sell them.

Professor Sukenik made arrangements to examine the scrolls. He unwrapped one, and his hands began to shake as he read a few sentences. Later, in recalling the experience, he said, "I looked and looked, and I suddenly had the feeling that I was privileged by destiny to gaze upon a Hebrew scroll which had not been read for more than two thousand years."

Hour after hour went by as Professor Sukenik and his friend haggled at length with the Arab merchant. But at the end of the session, the two friends left the tumbledown building with three precious scrolls, wrapped in paper, tucked under the professor's arm.

No, the scrolls didn't end up lost in some Bedouin tent in the Judean desert. No, they did not end up as shoe leather. Thank God that these ancient parchments made their way into the right hands.

I believe we see the hand of divine providence in the dramatic story of the Dead Sea Scroll discoveries. But the documents themselves give us an even more impressive picture of that providence. They demonstrate the extent to which the text of Scripture has been accurately preserved down through the centuries.

How?

Take the Isaiah scroll, for example. It was part of the largest single find in Qumran. In 1952, Cave 4 yielded a great treasure: thousands of fragments from 570 documents, including most of the Hebrew Bible. In fact, the entire book of Isaiah was there.

This gave scholars a historic opportunity. The Isaiah scroll was a thousand years *older* than the oldest Bible manuscripts heretofore available to translators. Scholars had a chance to compare the text in the Isaiah scroll with manuscripts copied a thousand years later. And the questions were: How much had the text been altered over the centuries? How close was the Bible in our hands to the words originally penned by the prophets? Were they the same?

What did the scholars come up with after their comparison? They found thirteen minor variations in the entire text—none of which significantly affect the meaning of any passage! Think of it! Only thirteen minor variations during one thousand years of copying and transmitting the words of Isaiah!

This amazing demonstration of accuracy led even reserved, cautious scholars to speak admiringly of the text. Dr. Don Carson wrote: "The scrolls tend to confirm the solidarity of our Old Testament to a greater degree than most people expected."

What the Dead Sea Scrolls have revealed about Bible manuscripts sheds new light on a marvelous promise in the Psalms:

> The words of the Lord are pure words, like silver tried in a furnace of earth, purified seven times. You shall keep them, O Lord, you shall preserve them from this generation forever (Psalm 12:6, 7, NKJV).

Yes, God's words *have* been preserved over the centuries, generation to generation, manuscript to manuscript. Why? Because those words are the pure words of truth, purified in a furnace seven times. God's hand guided the authors of Scripture as they chronicled His story, His principles. That same hand superintended those who copied and preserved the Scriptures for us.

Friend, the Bible isn't just a common book. It isn't some ordinary human philosophy. It's a divine document. In more than three thousand places the Bible declares itself to be inspired. Here is one clear example: "All Scripture is given by inspiration of God" (2 Timothy 3:16, NKJV). When you read the Bible, you are reading God's message to humanity; you are entering into a story that sweeps up every human being on this planet.

The Bible is more than just scrolls and parchments; it's even more than just authentic history. God's Word contains words of eternal life. Every book has a central character and a central theme. And the leading character in the whole Bible is Jesus Christ. The central theme of Scripture is how you and I can receive eternal life through Him.

In its pages we find God's own loving and forthright way of dealing with the sin problem—through Jesus. And, friend, it makes a difference what we believe about that. Either the Bible is telling the truth, or it isn't! Either Jesus is the Son of the living God, or He isn't. Either He died on the cross, or He didn't! Either Christ's offer of eternal life is real, or it isn't!

Some people say to me, "Pastor Finley, how can you get excited about the Dead Sea Scrolls? Who cares what someone wrote thousands of years ago—except for museum curators and rusty old university scholars?"

I'll tell you why I care. These ancient writings reveal Jesus. That's the only reason. Not only do they prophesy about Jesus, foretelling His life and death for me, but they *validate* that He truly was the Messiah and Saviour for you and me today.

I hope you realize now that God has gone to great lengths to help us believe the trustworthiness of the Bible. That's the good news echoing out of the caves of Qumran. We can trust every "thus saith the Lord." And we can have faith in the Christ of the Bible!

14 WHEN FAITH CRUMBLES

Do you sometimes find yourself caught in a sea of moral confusion? Do you wonder if it's possible to find truth? The Bible provides sane, sensible, proven answers to the deepest questions of human life. It's not a confusing book, difficult to understand. The God who loves you reveals truth clearly and personally.

If you've never studied the Bible before, or if your relationship with your Lord has been slipping, I suggest you begin by reading the Gospel of John. John's Gospel reveals Christ's compassion, forgiveness, and tender mercy—blended with His transforming love and incredible, life-changing power. As you follow Jesus' steps through Judea and Galilee, you will get to know Him—and you will begin to see what a powerful impact He has on every individual who opens up to His presence.

Consider Lew Wallace. When Wallace was practicing law in the midwestern United States, an atheist friend told him that within a few years all the little white churches dotting the Indiana countryside would be only a memory. Religion had no future.

Lew Wallace didn't know what to say. He realized, with a start, that he knew almost nothing about God or the Bible. He had no convictions on the subject. At that point, he determined to study the matter firsthand for himself. He decided to examine the Bible, using his legal training to look for credible evidence and reach proper conclusions.

Since he supposed this would be a rather dreary study, Wallace thought he might add some interest by creating a story about Jesus out of the materials he uncovered. At first he intended to present Him as a man, an extraordinary man to be sure, but just a human being. However, as he studied the historical background of Jesus' life and looked at the narratives in the Gospels, Wallace began seeing much more than he bargained for. The story he found in the Bible had a more-than-human design. The more he studied, the more convinced he became of the divinity of Christ. Certainly the world needed a Saviour, and Wallace couldn't imagine a better one than this Jesus.

So in his study Wallace found not only a story; he found God. He did go on to write the intended story about Christ, in part to express his new convictions. He called it *Ben Hur*. It became a bestselling novel and was later turned into one of Hollywood's biggest motion pictures.

The discoveries that changed Lew Wallace's life can be your discoveries too. Christ's love can be yours. His power can change your life. He longs for you to come to Him. He's waiting to reveal Himself to you in His Word—His *sure* Word verified by the old rolled-up scrolls found in the dusty hills beside the Dead Sea. Best of all, God is eager to accept you, forgive you, and change you.

Why not come to Him right now as we pray.

* * *

"Father mine, thank You for revealing Yourself in Your Word. Thank You for giving us the confidence that we can trust Your Word. The discoveries of the centuries reveal its accuracy. But, my Father, we especially thank You for Jesus, who came to live and die to make it possible one day for us to live with You forever. We accept His love right now. In Jesus' name. Amen."

A Life Written Beforehand

Of all the faces that stand out in history or the faces that flash through the media today, you've probably picked your favorites. The people who most inspire or fascinate you, personalities that shine above the crowd. As we deal with our share of weariness, boredom, or disappointment, it's nice to have heroes to admire.

But chances are, someone, somewhere is digging up facts that will throw a dark shadow over your favorite face. Chances are, if you knew the whole story, you wouldn't have too many heroes to hang on to. In recent years, many people who've seemed larger than life have been cut down to size by some formidable biographies. Take President Lyndon Baines Johnson, for example. He has become widely admired as the man most responsible for the civil rights legislation of the early sixties that helped break the back of racial injustice in the United States.

But now a new multivolume biography by Robert Caro paints a far more disturbing portrait of the man. Lyndon Johnson's moral courage in championing the cause of the poor and standing fast against stubborn segregationists is evident. But as the story of this ambitious man unfolds, we also see how ruthless he could be. In the second volume, *Means of Ascent*, Mr. Caro presents in devastating detail the record of how Johnson stole the Senate election in Texas, using every trick in the book—and making up some of his own. Thousands of votes for Johnson were simply manufactured. As Robert Caro completes his massive work, our picture of President Johnson will no doubt be more complete. But his stature may well be diminished at the same time.

Exhaustive biographies can be hard on heroes. All the flaws are revealed. The dark side frequently emerges. Often they leave us less sure of what to believe or admire. Heroes unmasked. Icons laid bare. We seem to be uncomfortable around anyone who appears larger than life. He or she must be cut down to size, to be no better than the rest of us. We seem to have lost our appetite for the heroic, the transcendent. And this attitude, I believe, has infected the religious life as well. We don't seem to want to worship a God who's too big, too authoritative. We seem more comfortable with a deity who's more manageable.

Take Jesus, for example. Calling Him the Son of God or seeing Him as the Saviour of the world doesn't come across too well these days. We would much rather see Him simply as a man—a good man, of course, a great moral teacher. Scholars take pains to present Him in the most human light possible. We can't grasp the possibility that the poor Rabbi wandering around Galilee could actually be God Himself in human form.

We don't want Him larger than life. And in many minds, Jesus has definitely been cut down to a human size. People today are asking, Is Jesus really any different from the founders of other religions—Buddha, Confucius, or Mohammed? They all have their teachings, their multitudes of followers; they all seem good and sincere.

This is, in fact, one of the great questions facing us today. How does Jesus fit into the grand scheme of things? How do we know whether His claims about Himself are true? Could

18 WHEN FAITH CRUMBLES

this man from Nazareth who lived two thousand years ago really be the one and only Son of God?

In a conversation with two disciples on the road to Emmaus, Jesus Himself points us toward one of the most compelling evidences of His divinity. These two men had become discouraged after news reached them of Christ's crucifixion. They'd begun to wonder if the One they'd followed so devotedly really was the Messiah. They questioned whether anyone so publicly humiliated and executed by the Romans could be the Son of God.

They were gloomily discussing these things when a stranger joined them on the road. They didn't recognize Him as Jesus. Jesus was the last person they expected to encounter. But He began talking to them; He began restoring their faith. And this is how Christ did it. Before He opened their eyes and let them see His glory, before He revealed Himself physically to their startled sense, He did this: "Beginning with Moses and all the Prophets, he explained to them what was said in all the Scriptures concerning himself" (Luke 24:27).

What did Jesus do for these despairing men? He began to read them His life story, written thousands of years before He was born. He quoted verse after verse from the Old Testament, specific predictions regarding the Messiah. And these two men realized that the details of their Master's life and death conformed exactly to these prophecies. His life had been written beforehand.

You know, each of us can have that same experience. By reading that biography, we can feel the awe those two disciples felt. That is one of the things that is utterly unique about Jesus Christ. His biography was written before He was born. We know it was completed, at the very latest, 250 years before His birth, because the Septuagint, the Greek translation of the Old Testament, existed at that time.

Let's look at just a few of the highlights of this unique

A LIFE WRITTEN BEFOREHAND 19

biography. It's sort of like putting together a puzzle. We'll compare predictions in the Old Testament with facts from the New Testament Gospels. Let's start with the birth of Jesus—the first piece of the puzzle. The prophet Micah wrote: " 'You, Bethlehem Ephrathah ... out of you will come for me one who will be ruler over Israel, whose origins are from of old, from ancient times' " (Micah 5:2).

Micah said the Messiah, the eternal ruler, would come from Bethlehem; he isolated that one town from all the other cities of Israel. As it turns out, the New Testament account fits right into this piece of the story. Luke 2:1-7 tells how Joseph and Mary had to travel to Bethlehem for a census and how their Child Jesus was born there.

The prophet Isaiah added to the picture. He predicted this: " 'The virgin will be with child and will give birth to a son, and will call him Immanuel' " (Isaiah 7:14). Matthew informs us that is just what happened. Look at Matthew 1:18, 22, 23. The virgin Mary conceived the Christ Child before she was taken as Joseph's wife.

The next piece of the puzzle is related to the timing of Christ's ministry to the world. Did you know that five hundred years before that historic event, a prophecy was given that actually predicted the very year in which our Lord would begin His ministry? We read the divine forecast in the book of Daniel:

> Seventy weeks are determined upon thy people and upon thy holy city. . . . Know therefore and understand, that from the going forth of the commandment to restore and to build Jerusalem unto the Messiah the Prince shall be seven weeks, and threescore and two weeks (Daniel 9:24, 25, KJV).

Let's do a little calculating. "Seven weeks, and three-

20 WHEN FAITH CRUMBLES

score and two weeks" equals sixty-nine weeks. Counting seven days to a week, we have 483 days. Now the Bible gives us a key to unlock symbolic prophecy. Numbers 14:34 and Ezekiel 4:6 suggest that one prophetic day is equal to one actual year. So, we are to look for 483 years to elapse between the decree to restore and rebuild Jerusalem and the time when Jesus would begin His ministry, or as Daniel puts it, be anointed as "Messiah the Prince" (verse 25).

This predicted decree to rebuild Jerusalem was issued in 457 B.C. by King Artaxerxes. It went into effect in the fall of that year. If we count forward 483 years from the date 457 B.C., guess where we end up? At the year 27 A.D. Precisely in the fall of that year, Jesus was baptized and the Holy Spirit descended on Him, anointing Him as the promised Messiah. You can read about this significant event in Luke 3:21-23. From that moment Jesus began His public ministry.

During the last twenty-four hours of Jesus' life, scores of prophecies, some a thousand years old, met their fulfillment. Take, for instance, His betrayal. The prophet Zechariah took up this part of the story. He predicted the actual price the betrayer would receive and what the money would be used for. In Zechariah 11:12, 13 we can almost hear the echo of Judas's harsh voice:

> I told them, "If you think it best, give me my pay; but if not, keep it." So they paid me thirty pieces of silver. And the Lord said to me, "Throw it to the potter." . . . So I took the thirty pieces of silver and threw them into the house of the Lord to the potter.

More than five hundred years later, Matthew related just how Judas Iscariot sealed his bargain with the priests, the enemies of Jesus. You can find the account in Matthew

A LIFE WRITTEN BEFOREHAND   21

27:3-10. Judas betrayed his Lord, not for twenty-five pieces of silver, not for twenty-eight or twenty-nine, but for exactly thirty pieces of silver. Then Judas realized, in a moment of anguish after Christ's arrest, that his terrible crime was not worth the price. The blood money was too heavy to bear. So he made his way to the temple, crying, "I have sinned. I have betrayed innocent blood." He tried to give the money back, but the priests refused it. So Judas threw the silver coins on the temple floor and went out to hang himself.

The priests now presumed to have scruples about placing this money in the temple treasury. So they used it to buy a field for paupers' graves. They bought a potter's field, a place that had been used for potters' workshops. So the details fell into place, just as Zechariah's contribution to the biography had foretold—thirty pieces of silver thrown into the Lord's house to the potter.

After Christ's betrayal came the ordeal of crucifixion. And this part of Jesus' life did not escape the notice of that ancient biography. Psalm 22:14, 16-18, for example, gives us an incredibly graphic portrayal of Christ's suffering on the cross. Listen to these words of agony:

> I am poured out like water, and all my bones are out of joint. My heart has turned to wax; it has melted away within me. . . . They have pierced my hands and my feet. I can count all my bones; people stare and gloat over me. They divide my garments among them and cast lots for my clothing.

Here we see in detail the trauma of the cross. Christ's hands and feet were pierced with nails; hanging on the cross, His shoulders were pulled out of joint; He could look down and see His rib cage jutting out. When the soldier pierced His side, blood and water poured out. The specific statement in verse 16 about His hands and feet being pierced is validated by a remarkable New Testament passage in which the disciples actually touched the wounds in Christ's body (see John 20:25-27).

Psalm 22:18 predicts that Jesus' garments would be divided among those putting Him to death. This found a remarkable fulfillment. Notice that verse 18 describes both dividing His garments and casting lots for them. According to Roman custom, the meager belongings of a condemned person became the property of His executioners. So at the crucifixion, the Roman soldiers divided up Christ's clothes among them. But then one soldier noticed Christ's seamless robe. To divide it would be to destroy it. So the practical suggestion was made that they cast lots for the robe. Without knowing it, the Roman soldiers were fulfilling Bible prophecy with an accuracy that demonstrates their victim was indeed the Messiah, the promised Redeemer. Even the act of those Roman soldiers gambling for His clothes at the foot of the cross (see Matthew 27:35) was part of that biography penned so long before the events happened.

Yes, the pieces of the puzzle fit together. When we look closely at that story written so long ago, we see that it forms a picture, a magnificent painting of Jesus Christ. Amazingly enough, the brush strokes were laid down by Hebrew prophets thousands of years before their subject could sit for a portrait.

The biography of Jesus was written in incredible detail before He was born! But there is another reason His biography is unique in the history of humankind. Unlike all the other stories of great men and women who have walked this planet, the life of Jesus does not end with His death. The Gospels come to a climax not with the crucifixion, but with the account of His resurrection verified by

A LIFE WRITTEN BEFOREHAND 23

eyewitnesses including His closest disciples. Jesus is still alive, and His life is continually being reproduced in the hearts of men and women today. His life is not just a static record of past wonders; it continues supernaturally. The Messiah is still very much alive, turning hopeless cases of crushed humanity into an extension of His own glorious biography.

Don't you want to be part of that story—the story that was written about thousands of years ago? The story that became flesh and blood in the person of Jesus Christ? The story that continues today in the lives of men and women who accept Him as their Saviour?

No matter how dark your past or how uncertain your future, Christ can bring you into His victorious life. He can replace your weaknesses with His strengths. And He can offer you a new beginning through His forgiveness and love. Become a part of the greatest story every told now, as we pray.

* * *

"Dear Father, thank You for guiding the hands of those writers of Scripture who have brought us the good news about Jesus. Thank You for demonstrating its truth through the accuracy of prophecy. Right now, we want to accept Your Son, who died on the cross as our Saviour and Lord. We want to commit our lives to Him and walk with Him from this day forward. Thank You for Your redeeming grace. Amen."

If God Is So Good...

The brave infantryman who'd made it through seven months of Desert Shield and Desert Storm had lasted less than twenty-four hours back home in Detroit. He'd been murdered on the street in cold blood, cut down in the prime of life.

Army Specialist Anthony Riggs was well liked among the men of Delta Battery, who'd been assigned to shoot down Scud missiles over the Arabian desert. He was friendly and a hard worker. His buddies called him "Light Bulb."

Light Bulb didn't know what it was to rush for cover. He had a special kind of confidence. In one of his letters home, he wrote, "There's no way I'm going to die in this . . . country. With the Lord's grace and His guidance, I'll walk American soil again." Anthony's trust in God wasn't just a reflex under fire. He'd been part of a gospel singing group in the States. His pastor thought of him as a warm and gentle man, "the kind of person who met his challenges and faced them happily."

Well, Anthony Riggs did survive the war and was welcomed home as one of its heroes. On the day following his night flight home, he began packing a rental van with his wife's belongings. Drug dealers had moved into their neighborhood in northeast Detroit, and Anthony planned to move his wife and stepdaughter, Amber, to a better place in the suburbs.

That evening he played with Amber and then took a nap. Awake from jet lag around two o'clock in the morning, he decided to take a last load out to the van. Shortly afterward, five shots rang out. A neighbor rushed out to see Anthony Riggs sprawled face down with his head against the curb. The soldier who had survived Desert Storm gasped for air, coughed, and died in the dark.

It seemed such a tragic, meaningless act. Here was a man who'd performed bravely on the field of battle; he'd survived Scud missiles raining down from the night sky. He'd shown himself a responsible, hard-working young man with a bright future. He seemed to be a sincere Christian.

And people asked, Why him, of all people? Why Anthony Riggs? There seems to be no good answer to those shots ringing out in the dark. So many others are struck down, and so many others leave us with the same question: Why?

We see children withering away with leukemia and ask: Why? We see families scarred for life because of an alcoholic parent and ask: Why? We see corruption, starvation, oppression, and we wonder: If God is good, why is the world so bad? If God really loves His children, why do so many suffer so terribly?

Today, I'd like to share with you a very important answer to that question. It's not the whole answer, but it's something that is often overlooked. I believe a parable Jesus told helps us understand the origin of our woes and helps to answer that question: Why?

Jesus talked about a field that was perfectly tilled and prepared for seed. He pictured a good man who planted seed in the field and who was looking forward to an abundant harvest. But some time later a servant dis-

26 WHEN FAITH CRUMBLES

covered that useless weeds had popped up everywhere among the wheat and asked, " 'Sir, didn't you sow good seed in your field? Where then did the weeds come from?' " (Matthew 13:27).

That's the question every human being faces at some time in life. If God is good, if He made this world blossom for His children, why do we see so many tragic weeds?

In Jesus' parable, the master answered that question very simply. He said, " 'An enemy did this' " (verse 28). Where does suffering come from? Where do sickness and heartache and anxiety come from? Jesus' answer is: "They didn't happen because of the master of the field; he planted it with good seed. He didn't sow sickness and suffering and death. It was an enemy, an enemy of God and humans, who came in the night and sowed his seeds of destruction."

The Bible consistently identifies this enemy as Satan, a being who rebelled against God and unleashed the whole sin problem. In Scripture, the devil isn't just some fairy-tale figure who flits around with a pitchfork. He is a very real being who causes very real tragedies.

How did it all get started? The prophet Ezekiel actually gives us a picture of Satan's downfall in his description of a certain haughty king. Chapter 28 speaks of a being who was "the model of perfection, full of wisdom." He'd been ordained "a guardian cherub" who walked among the fiery stones "on the holy mount of God" (verses 12, 14). But something happened to this mighty angel known as Lucifer. Verse 17 says, "Your heart became proud on account of your beauty, and you corrupted your wisdom because of your splendor" (NIV). Pride made Lucifer stumble in heaven.

Why? Was God responsible for some defect in his character? No. Ezekiel refers to this angel as "blameless in your ways from the day you were created" (verse 15). But God did create beings with the capacity to choose. He didn't want angelic beings to obey Him only because they were forced to do so. He didn't want robots marching around with head erect and shoulders back, directed by some cosmic control center. God wanted worship given freely from hearts of love, from minds that appreciated His character. But here's the catch. If individuals really have the right to choose, then they can make wrong choices. They can decide *not* to love God.

And that's just what Lucifer did. He indulged in pride. He began to envy the power of God and instigated a rebellion. The prophet Isaiah tells us about the tragic results:

> How you have fallen from heaven, O morning star, son of the dawn! You have been cast down to the earth. . . . You said in your heart, "I will ascend to heaven; I will raise my throne above the stars of God. . . . I will make myself like the Most High" (Isaiah 14:12-14).

Lucifer made wrong choices. He had the freedom to do that. But God is no more responsible for Lucifer's choice to sin than He's responsible for drunkenness because He created grapes. This, however, brings us to another question. "If God is loving, if He knew that Satan was going to bring such misery to the universe, why didn't He destroy him in the beginning as soon as he sinned?"

Well, the fact is, God could have destroyed Lucifer as soon as he started having those envious thoughts. He could have nipped rebellion in the bud. But think for a moment of what that would have said to all the other watching angels. An illustration from government may help us understand. Imagine that the president of the United States, sitting in his Oval Office in Washington, has come under attack by a powerful member of his cabinet. The cabinet member accuses him of being unfair, arbitrary, and dictatorial. He claims the president doesn't really have the citizens' interests in mind at all but is using his office to further his own selfish purposes.

Now, how should the president respond—if the charges are false? Suppose he called on an anti-terrorist squad from the CIA to track down the cabinet member and kill him? Would that clear his name? What if he ordered National Guard units to surround the man at his home and do away with him? Would that solve the problem?

You see the point, of course. God's reputation and credibility were at stake when Satan delivered his haughty challenge. The question raised was: "Is God really just? Is His way really best?" Eradicating the opposition wouldn't have answered that challenge.

Instead, God chose a wiser course. He would allow sin to exist in the universe for a period of time. He would wait until it had been fully demonstrated that rebellion against Him does not bring happiness, but rather sickness and disaster. He would wait until the whole universe could see that God's way brings joy and Lucifer's way brings only death. Then, and only then, would God destroy all evil.

So Lucifer was allowed to carry out his alternative plan. But this brings up yet another question. How did planet Earth get involved? Was it created simply as a dumping ground for Satan? Were human beings destined to suffer under his dominion?

The book of Genesis tells us that everything was "good" when God created this world (see Genesis 1:31), and that included the first human beings. Everything was perfect in Eden. But God made human beings with the power of free choice, just as He had created the angels free to choose.

When Eve wandered over to the forbidden Tree of the Knowledge of Good and Evil, Satan, disguised as a serpent, had the opportunity to spread his lies. Eve told him that

God said she would die if she ate the fruit of this tree. But Satan replied: " 'You will not surely die. . . . For God knows that when you eat of it your eyes will be opened, and you will be like God, knowing good and evil' " (Genesis 3:4, 5).

After Adam and Eve ate of the forbidden tree, they were filled with guilt and anxiety. When God came looking for them in the garden, they hid from His face, and humanity has been running and hiding ever since. Sin produces alienation between us and God, alienation between people. The seeds of Satan's war against God were planted in the hearts of the parents of the human race when they sinned. That's the reason there is abuse in the home, the reason there is violence in the streets, the reason there is so much animosity in this world—sin has infected the human heart.

In short, Satan's alternative produces death. Every gravestone we see is a testament to his big lie: " 'You will not surely die' " (verse 4). Sin produces physical death, emotional death, and spiritual death. But God didn't abandon us to our fate because we rebelled against Him. From the very beginning, when sin first entered our world, He had a plan. He has shown us a way out. God gave this message of warning to Satan, speaking to the serpent: " 'I will put enmity between you and the woman, and between your offspring and hers; he will crush your head, and you will strike his heel' " (verse 15).

How would this happen?

It would happen through the promised offspring of the woman, Jesus Christ. He would come and crush the serpent's head at the cross; He would destroy the oppressive power of Satan.

Have you ever wondered, "Why doesn't God do something about the sickness and sin and heartache in our world?" The answer is, He *has* done something. In the gift of His Son, He's given us everything necessary to restore us from sin and its terrible results. Jesus has delivered us

30 WHEN FAITH CRUMBLES

from the penalty of sin, and He can give us the ability to live triumphantly, even in a world dominated by sin.

I began this chapter with the tragedy of Anthony Riggs. I'd like to end with the triumph of John McCain. Like Anthony, John was also involved in a war. He was a pilot in Vietnam. He spent five and a half years as a prisoner of war in Hanoi, where he and other pilots endured terrible suffering.

But there was one day, John remembers clearly—a day when he and his fellow prisoners were able to rise above the abuse and isolation. It was Christmas Eve, 1971. A few days earlier, John had been allowed to have a Bible for just a few moments. He furiously copied down as many verses of the Christmas story as he could.

Now, on this special night—Christmas Eve—the men had decided to have their own Christmas service. They began with the Lord's Prayer. Then they sang Christmas carols, and McCain read a portion of Luke's Gospel after each hymn. The men were nervous. They remembered the time, about a year earlier, when the guards had burst in on their secret church service and started beating the three men who were leading prayers. They had dragged these three away to solitary confinement; the rest of the prisoners had been shut up in three-by-five-foot cells for eleven months.

Still, the prisoners wanted to sing on this day. Barely above a whisper, they began singing, "O come, all ye faithful, joyful and triumphant," their eyes glancing anxiously at the barred windows. As the service progressed, the prisoners grew bolder; they lifted their voices a little higher until they filled the cell with "Hark! the Herald Angels Sing" and "It Came Upon the Midnight Clear." Some of the men were too sick to stand, but others propped them up and placed blankets around their trembling shoulders. Everyone wanted to join in the songs that made them feel joyful and triumphant.

When they came to "Silent Night," tears rolled down their unshaven faces. As John McCain later wrote, "Suddenly we were two thousand years and half a world away in a village called Bethlehem. And neither war, nor torture, nor imprisonment had dimmed the hope born on that silent night so long before."

As the prisoners in that North Vietnamese cell sang with feeling the final refrain, "Sleep in heavenly peace, sleep in heavenly peace," they realized that a transformation had taken place. John said: "We had forgotten our wounds, our hunger, our pain. We raised prayers of thanks for the Christ Child, for our families and homes. There was an absolutely exquisite feeling that our burdens had been lifted. In a place designed to turn men into vicious animals, we clung to one another, sharing what comfort we had."

What words of comfort can we share in this world that Satan has overgrown with so many tragic weeds of sin? We can lift up a song of triumph. We can lift up a song of defiance against the enemy who "came and sowed weeds" (Matthew 13:25). We can sing because we know that God has bound up His life with ours. He has come into the world and suffered with us. And someday we will triumph with Him.

* * *

"Father, we're often perplexed by the cruelty and randomness of life. We're sometimes tempted to blame You. But help us now to understand who is really responsible for these things, and help us to turn from the enemy who has planted all these weeds in our lives and in our world. We accept Your Son as our Saviour and Lord. We trust in the name of Jesus from this day forward. Amen."

Why Millions Are Not Christians

Northern Ireland has been making headlines in recent years because of deep, abiding hatreds that compel people to lob bombs into crowded restaurants, gun down women and children, and cripple informers by shooting them through the kneecaps. Northern Ireland is all about Catholics and Protestants at war with one another. It's a Christian scandal—and the whole world knows about it. People claiming to be followers of Jesus have become terrorists!

For years, Lebanon has been racked by bloody civil war too—car bombings, cruel reprisals, and endless street fighting. Who are the protagonists? Shiite Muslims and Maronite Christians—conducting endless bloodshed in the name of religion!

How can loyalty to a particular religious faith make people actually kill one another? It isn't a new phenomenon. It happened in Bible times; it happened in the infamous Crusades; it happened during the fearful Inquisition. And it's happening now.

Is it any wonder that millions of people see the cross of Christianity as a threat, not as a hope of salvation? Who in their right mind wants to be a part of all this mayhem?

In this chapter, I don't want to just talk about the

WHY MILLIONS ARE NOT CHRISTIANS   33

problem; I'd like to explore a solution. I believe there is a definite kind of religious belief that tends toward intolerance and bloodshed. And I believe there's a definite kind of religious belief that moves us in the opposite direction. There *is* something that can make Christianity compelling for all people everywhere. And one day on a hill in Galilee, Jesus showed us exactly what that thing is.

It was near Capernaum that Christ gave the first public declaration of what His kingdom was all about. It was something like a president's inaugural address in which he lays out his vision of where he wants the country to go, what he thinks it can achieve.

Jesus, accompanied as always by His closest disciples, went to a spot overlooking the lake where He could be heard by the multitude. Here, echoing down the green slopes of Galilee and out toward the blue, rippled surface of the lake, the Master Teacher's words fell on fishermen, farmers, merchants, scribes, and priests. It was Jesus' greatest discourse. And Matthew, sitting there with the other disciples at the feet of the Saviour, made sure that it would echo down through the years to us. He compressed Jesus' sermon—the world's most profound moral insights—into chapters 5, 6, and 7 of his Gospel. In the Sermon on the Mount, Jesus unveiled the kind of religion that forms the basis of His kingdom—the kind of religion that would win over the whole world.

Just what kind of religion is it that shines through this sermon? I suggest it is essentially this: God's law written in human hearts. Jesus wanted to revolutionize religion by taking it from the outside and placing it on the inside.

He opened with blessings—the Beatitudes, we call them—on certain kinds of people who, He said, would inherit the kingdom of heaven. Who are these people? Jesus mentioned the poor in spirit, the pure in heart, the meek and merciful, and those who hunger and thirst for righteousness. The characteristics Jesus commended are largely invisible qualities. You can't put your finger on purity of heart. You can't exactly pin down what constitutes a heart longing for righteousness. These are internal, spiritual traits.

Unfortunately, these are also precisely the traits that many religious people overlook. We instinctively focus on externals; it's human nature. We go to a certain church; we nod through a certain worship ritual; we sign on the dotted line below doctrines—and that's our religion. Think about it. When someone says they belong to a certain denomination, how do we respond? "Oh, that's the church that doesn't use music." "Oh, that's the church where the ministers walk around in robes." "Oh, the members of that church don't eat meat." The externals are what click in our minds. The internal qualities—well, they're harder to grasp.

But Jesus' Sermon on the Mount zeroes in on things that can happen only in the human heart. Listen to how He expanded on the law. The Master pointed to the command that says, "Do not murder" (see Exodus 20:13). Then He warned of being angry with your brother and abusing him. Why? Because that's where murder starts; that's where the problem must be dealt with—in the anger that simmers in our hearts.

What's the religion of Christ all about? I believe Matthew 6:19-21 gives a good summary:

> "Do not store up for yourselves treasures on earth.... But store up for yourselves treasures in heaven.... For where your treasure is, there your heart will be also."

Where our heart is—that's what matters. Have we focused on the external things around us, even external religious things? Or is our investment in the qualities of

WHY MILLIONS ARE NOT CHRISTIANS   35

heaven—the imperishable commodities of purity and unselfishness?

We desperately need this kind of religion of the heart today. This is the only kind of faith that can win over the world. People in Northern Ireland are fighting largely because religion has become focused on the outside. Religion has become a political tool; it's about who controls what neighborhood; it's about who has the most economic leverage. It's about parades up and down the streets, showing off the externals of one's faith as a challenge to the opposition. I can guarantee you it's not about being pure in heart or hungering and thirsting for righteousness.

Why have Christians and Muslims been fighting in Lebanon so long? For the same reason. They have been wearing their religion on their sleeves. Faith has become a battle over turf. You plant a banner of faith in a certain neighborhood in order to own it, in order to shore up your political power.

Religion that is all on the outside is a complete disaster, my friends. And that's what Jesus came to change. He came to put religious faith inside, where it belongs. I believe that kind of faith can change the world.

Jesus became quite specific about what His religion of the heart would do. If love is welling up inside our hearts, instead of anger; if generosity is welling up inside, instead of pride; if a longing for righteousness consumes us, instead of a longing for more possessions—then amazing things will start to happen.

Jesus actually suggested that if a bad-tempered person strikes us on the right cheek, we should turn to him our left cheek! If someone wants our tunic, we should offer him our cloak as well! Those people on the Galilean hillside must have found Jesus' words about loving their enemies the hardest to take. "It's easy to love your family and friends," Jesus told them. "The thing that really demonstrates genuine religion is to show love for your enemies."

This Sermon on the Mount, given two thousand years ago, is starting to look humanly unattainable. Everything Jesus said in His sermon goes against human nature. It's natural to want to hit back, not to turn the other cheek. It's natural to desire the blessings of riches and high position, not the blessedness of the meek and poor in spirit. It's natural to point to the speck in our brother's eye, not deal with the log in our own. It's natural to hate our enemies, not to pray for them.

We simply can't do the things Jesus asks of us. He might as well have commanded us to walk on water. But maybe that's part of His point.

Remember that Jesus emphasized a heart religion—the law written inside us. Well, the prophets, too, had promised that God would write His law in our hearts. Under the new covenant, He would take out our hearts of stone and give us hearts of flesh.

Jesus' Sermon on the Mount is not something we just drift into naturally. It demands a supernatural religion. Only the Spirit of the living God dwelling inside us can produce these amazing qualities that Jesus talked about.

I think it's interesting that Jesus gave His sermon while overlooking the Lake of Galilee, the site of so many of His miracles. Here is where He miraculously multiplied fish in the nets of His disciples. Here is where He calmed a raging storm. Yes, here is where Jesus walked on water.

That's the point. We can't walk on water, but Jesus can. We can't fulfill His idealistic religion, but He can. Jesus can write His new law in our hearts. And when that happens, believe me, my friends, we can do the impossible!

Late one evening during World War II, three men conversed in a small flat in Bucharest—Richard Wurmbrand, a Lutheran pastor; his landlord; and Borila, a soldier on leave from the front, where Romania was fighting as a

WHY MILLIONS ARE NOT CHRISTIANS 37

German ally. Borila dominated the conversation, boasting of his adventures in battle and especially of how he had volunteered to help exterminate Jews in a Romanian border province, killing hundreds with his own hands.

Wurmbrand realized with horror that his own wife's family had been murdered at the camps there. This man, bragging before him, may well have been their murderer! He was filled with indignation. But as they continued talking, something else began to fill his heart. Wurmbrand himself had lived a godless life before being converted through reading about Christ's life in the Gospels. The teachings of Jesus had overwhelmed him. And one of the things Jesus taught was to love one's enemies.

Wurmbrand began to see in this cruel soldier someone Jesus was trying to save. So he invited Borila to his apartment to listen to some of the Ukrainian melodies he said he liked. At the apartment, Wurmbrand began playing the piano—softly, so as not to awaken his wife and baby son. After a bit, he could see the soldier was moved by the music. He stopped playing and said, "If you look through that curtain, you can see someone asleep in the next room. It's my wife, Sabina. Her parents, her sisters, and her twelve-year-old brother have been killed along with others of the family. You told me that you have killed hundreds of Jews at the camp where my wife's family was taken. You don't know yourself whom you have killed, so we can assume that you are the murderer of her family."

Borila leaped from his chair, eyes blazing, looking as if he could strangle the pastor. But Wurmbrand calmed him and proposed an experiment: "I shall wake my wife and tell her who you are and what you have done. I can tell you what will happen. My wife will not speak one word of reproach! She'll embrace you as if you were her brother. She will prepare food for you—the best things she has in the house." Then Pastor Wurmbrand made his appeal: "If my wife, a sinner as we all are, can forgive and love like this, imagine how Jesus, who is perfect love, can forgive and love you!" He urged the soldier to turn to God and ask for forgiveness.

Borila's heart melted. Rocking back and forth, he sobbed out his confession: "I'm a murderer; I'm soaked in blood...." Wurmbrand guided him to his knees and began praying; Borila, having no experience with prayer, simply begged for forgiveness over and over.

Then the pastor walked into the bedroom and gently awakened his wife. "There is a man here whom you must meet," he whispered. "We believe he has murdered your family, but he has repented, and now he is our brother."

Sabina came out in her dressing gown and extended her hands to the huge, tear-stained soldier. Both wept greatly, and amid the overwhelming emotions of grief, they embraced fervently. Finally, Sabina went into the kitchen to prepare some food.

Wurmbrand thought that his guest could use a further reinforcement of grace. So the pastor stepped into the next room and returned with his two-year-old son, Mihai, fast asleep in his arms. Borila was dismayed; only hours before he had boasted of killing Jewish children in their parents' arms. The sight of Wurmbrand's son seemed an unbearable reproach; he expected a withering rebuke. Instead, the pastor leaned forward and said, "Do you see how quietly he sleeps? You are like a newborn child who can rest in the Father's arms. The blood that Jesus shed has cleansed you." Looking down at Mihai, Borila felt a surge of pure happiness.

When this soldier rejoined his regiment, he laid aside his weapons and volunteered to rescue the wounded under fire. The Sermon on the Mount had been written in one more person's heart.

A church, built to commemorate Christ's Sermon on the Mount, overlooks the Lake of Galilee today. It is in the

WHY MILLIONS ARE NOT CHRISTIANS 39

shape of an octagon and has one of the Beatitudes inscribed on each of its eight sides. It's nice to build monuments of stone to this greatest of ethical discourses. But even more important is the monument Christ wants to build in your heart and mine. A religion turned from exterior things to interior qualities—God's law written in our hearts—that is the faith that can make all the difference in the world.

Mahatma Gandhi once remarked that if Christians would live the Sermon on the Mount, all India would follow Christ. That is what Jesus is calling every human being on this planet to do. Yes, Christ's ideals *are* attainable by His grace. He wants to put His ideals in our hearts. He wants to turn people who have lost their savor into the salt of the earth. He wants to turn people who are hiding under a bushel into the light of the world.

You can begin living the miraculous Sermon on the Mount right now. You can share the kind of faith that will win millions to the Master. Won't you invite Him into your heart now as we pray?

* * *

"Father, we thank You for giving us the beautiful principles of this great sermon. That's what life is all about. Yet we feel terribly weak and frail when confronted with Your ideals. And so we invite You into our lives as Saviour and as Lord. Thank You, first of all, for Your death on the cross—for the pardon that makes salvation possible. And thank You, also, for writing the law in our hearts through Your Holy Spirit. Keep us in close communion with You each day. Keep us open to the Spirit's writing each day. In the name of our Saviour. Amen."

A Tale of Two Tombs

Imagine you're one of Jesus Christ's disciples, and on that fateful Sunday morning you have heard wild rumors of a resurrection. Imagine you've come to the place where they laid Him. What would you notice, peering anxiously into that tomb carved into the stone? Would you have seen any evidence that the utterly impossible had really come to pass?

Many different religious leaders have arisen in history with many different claims about how to find peace, happiness, final truth, and salvation. Confucius claimed to teach the way to order and harmony between heaven and earth. Buddha claimed to show the way to transcend human suffering. Bahä Alläh, founder of Bahaism, claimed his truths synthesized all the world's faiths into one. But one religious leader made a claim more outlandish than any other. Only one actually claimed to have literally risen from the dead. Only one religion claims an empty tomb as its cornerstone.

That's why the resurrection of Jesus Christ has been one of the most controversial beliefs in all history. It isn't just a matter of what you feel in your heart. It isn't just a matter of religious symbolism or myth. It's a matter of: "Did He, or didn't He?" It's a question of historical evidence.

A TALE OF TWO TOMBS 41

In our hyperscientific world today, we are apt to be skeptical of any kind of religious claim—especially a supernatural one. We just don't see people rising from the grave these days. Everything we know about biology and anatomy tells us that it just can't happen.

But, obviously, the idea of Christ's resurrection has had an enormous impact on the world. So what are we to make of it? Is there any way to know what really occurred during those early hours on Sunday morning after Jesus' crucifixion? It happened so long ago. Is it just a matter of faith? Do we simply believe Jesus rose from the dead because that's what the Christian religion affirms?

In this chapter, I'd like to show you some rock-solid evidence that supports faith. You are going to discover that the resurrection is actually the best explanation for what we *know* happened just after the death of Christ. The resurrection explains certain established facts that no other theory can explain.

Let's begin with the facts that virtually all scholars agree on. Even scholars who do not accept the Bible as the Word of God have concluded that the envidence points to certain inescapable facts:

1. After a public crucifixion, Jesus died and was buried in a tomb.
2. Jesus' death caused His disciples to despair and lose hope.
3. The disciples had real experiences that they believed were literal appearances of the risen Jesus.
4. As a result, the disciples were transformed from fearful doubters to bold proclaimers.
5. The resurrection message was proclaimed in Jerusalem, where Jesus had died.
6. The church was born and grew dramatically.
7. Two skeptics, Paul and Jesus' brother, James, were

42 WHEN FAITH CRUMBLES

converted after seeing what they believed to be the risen Jesus.

Now, remember, these are not just statements of faith. These are the basic facts everyone can agree on. And these are facts that need to be accounted for. Why and how did these seven things happen? If Jesus really *did* rise from the grave, then all seven events are perfectly understandable.

But let's say that Jesus *did not* rise from the grave. Then, we have to come up with some other explanation for the disciples' faith and the growth of the church. Here are some of the theories that have been tried out.

One is that the disciples managed to steal the body of Christ. This theory was popularized in the book, *The Passover Plot*. It would explain why the tomb was found empty, and it would explain how the disciples could proclaim Christ was risen with the assurance that none of their enemies would be able to produce His body.

However, the Passover Plot runs straight into the Roman guard posted at the tomb of Christ. Imagine what had to happen if this theory is correct. The disciples, immediately after experiencing utter despair over the loss of their Master and the destruction of all their hopes, get together and decide to steal the body and concoct an enormous lie. Somehow, they sneak past the Roman guard. (Remember, these are disciplined soldiers who know they will pay with their lives if anything happens on their watch.) The disciples make off with Christ's body. Then they proceed to proclaim to all Jerusalem and the world that Christ has risen. They keep proclaiming this lie through hardship, toil, and persecution. Finally, they give their lives to maintain their lie.

I don't think so. The Passover Plot falls apart as soon as we take a closer look. Actually, it fell apart when it was first tried out by the Pharisees and Sadducees. They bribed

A TALE OF TWO TOMBS 43

some of the Roman guards to say the disciples had stolen the body while they were sleeping (see Matthew 28:11-15). While they were sleeping? If they were sleeping, how did they know it was the disciples who took the body?

Well, how about another explanation? How about the Hallucination Theory? It has been argued that Christ's appearances to His disciples after His death were really some kind of illusion. The disciples wanted to see Him again so badly that they imagined they did.

This theory runs smack into one simple fact: numbers. Christ didn't just appear to isolated individuals after His death; He appeared to *groups* of people. He walked into a room where the disciples were huddled in fear and despair. A risen Christ was the last thing on earth they expected to see. That's not all. Jesus also appeared to other groups. Five hundred people in all saw Christ alive after His crucifixion.

Now, a deeply disturbed person may indeed have some kind of hallucination that is very real to him. And various kinds of individuals in various kinds of suggestive states have various kinds of hallucinations. But the one thing the experts are agreed on is this: Several people don't all have the same hallucination at the same time.

A group of people *can* look up in the sky, see some kind of strange, bright light, and all conclude that it's a UFO. They can hear strange noises in a house or see unusual movements and conclude they've seen a ghost. But these are *not* hallucinations. These are simply a matter of interpreting ambiguous information.

Furthermore, as we've noted, the postresurrection appearances of Christ were *detailed* encounters. People interacted with Christ. At one point, the risen Christ even fixed His disciples breakfast on the shore of Lake Galilee. Now that would be some hallucination!

One by one, the classic attempts to explain away the resurrection have been discredited. Today, there is no clear

44 WHEN FAITH CRUMBLES

naturalistic theory for skeptics to cling to.

The evidence scholars have gathered for the resurrection has solidified like the great stone that blocked the entrance to the tomb. And so, people who still insist on disbelieving this remarkable event have pretty much settled on taking comfort in *distance*. They say, in effect, "Well, the alleged event was so very long ago. Who knows what really happened? Who knows whether the Gospel records are accurate or not? Maybe this idea of a resurrection gradually developed among early believers. They could have looked back and reinterpreted things that happened. Maybe the disciples at some point started talking about what *should* have happened instead of what really *did* happen."

First of all, this line of argument really begs the question. We've already pointed out that scholars today accept certain events related to Christ's death as demonstrated, knowable. And all of these facts make sense *only* if Christ really did rise from the grave.

Yet, let's look closely at this theory—the idea that the resurrection was part of a myth that gradually emerged in the early church. After all, it sounds plausible at first glance. We're all familiar with great men and women who became larger-than-life legends some time after their death. Maybe that's the way it was with Jesus. Maybe He was a good man, a great man, but His followers later turned Him into a superman who defied even death itself.

Well, here's some fascinating news. This theory runs smack into several remarkable inscriptions discovered in a tomb on the road to Bethlehem.

Some years ago, Professor E. L. Sukenik, a Jewish archaeologist, began excavating a Christian tomb in the dry limestone hills around Jerusalem. The tomb contained several stone boxes called *ossuaries* in which bones of the dead were placed. Professor Sukenik found markings on

A TALE OF TWO TOMBS 45

these ossuaries that led him to claim he'd found the earliest evidences of Christianity ever uncovered. On all four sides of one of the boxes, he found rough, charcoal-drawn crosses. He also found several Greek inscriptions on the ossuaries.

But what made this discovery particularly important was the age of the tomb. Broken bits of pottery found in the tomb are of a type known as "Herodian." And the tomb contained a dated coin minted by Agrippa I in the year A.D. 41; no coins or pottery of a later origin were found. So here we have evidence of Christian faith in the forties, only ten years or so after Christ's crucifixion in A.D. 31!

But now we come to the truly astounding discovery. Two ossuaries were inscribed with the name "Jesus." These were not the names of the persons whose bones were *in* the ossuary; rather, they were statements of faith, words of dedication. On one, the name of Jesus was followed by the Greek letters, *iou*, a shortened version of *Yahweh*, the name of God. What we have, then, on a tomb from the A.D. forties is an inscription that reads: *Jesus Yahweh*, or "Jesus is God."

But there's more! The other ossuary carrying the name of Jesus had the Greek letters *aloth* following it. This is simply a Hebrew word (*aloth*) written with Greek letters. It means "ascended one."

Do you grasp the significance of this? Within a few years of Jesus' death, people were burying their dead with these statements of faith chiseled in stone: "Jesus is God." "Jesus is the ascended one, the one who ascended." That's what these inscriptions in stone proclaim loud and clear. People believed in Jesus' divinity and resurrection right after He was crucified.

Do you know what this does to the Myth Theory, the idea that the resurrection of Jesus was a legend that somehow rose out of the history of the church? It buries it!

People were proclaiming the resurrection of Jesus Christ

in A.D. forty-something, while thousands who had known and seen Him were still alive and walking around. If Jesus the risen Saviour was a myth, it was the world's one-and-only instant myth.

The final nail in the coffin of the Myth Theory is this: People who had seen Christ alive after His burial were proclaiming His resurrection immediately afterward in Jerusalem—and no one could silence them. No one could silence them by producing Jesus' body.

One by one, the theories that attempt to explain away the resurrection have been shattered. Believe it or not, the resurrection of Christ is on firmer ground than ever before, even today in our skeptical, hyperscientific world. To all who will look carefully at the evidence, the resurrection is an almost-inescapable historical fact.

It is that fact—the resurrection—that distinguishes Christ from all other religious leaders, all other great figures of history. The Founder of Christianity is alive! What a different message His empty tomb proclaims than that of all the other great monuments in the world. I was deeply impressed by that thought during a recent visit to Moscow and Lenin's tomb in Red Square.

For decades, tens of thousands of people stood in line waiting to get into Lenin's tomb. Some waited for five or six hours; Lenin was a revered god to them. Today, the lines are gone; today, very few people come to see Lenin's tomb—just a few tourists. Today, visitors can walk in without having to wait at all.

In a different city is another tomb. That tomb is in Jerusalem, not Moscow. That tomb does not contain a body, because Jesus Christ is alive! Part of the reason that Communism has died in Russia and Christianity is bursting to live once again is very simple: the founder of Communism still lies in his grave; the Founder of Christianity rules from the skies. I saw the power of the living Christ very

A TALE OF TWO TOMBS 47

clearly as scores of people in the former Soviet Union came face to face with the gospel.

Today in Moscow, thousands stand in other lines. Not in lines to see Lenin's tomb, but in lines to receive a Bible; in lines to hear the gospel; in lines to get to know this Christ, who is alive. A dead leader cannot save anyone. Only a living leader, the living Saviour, Jesus Christ, can fully save.

Have you become acquainted with this living Saviour? Do you know Jesus Christ as a present companion—or simply as a great moral teacher from the distant past? You can begin a meaningful, personal relationship with Him right now. You can take the first step on a wonderful journey with the Christ who lives. Why not do that right now, as we pray?

* * *

"Heavenly Father, thank You for giving us the gift of Your Son. Thank You for giving us all these wonderful, specific evidences that Jesus really did conquer death as Saviour and Lord. We accept Him right now into our lives. Thank You for forgiving our sins, and thank You for accepting us into Your family. Help us now to enjoy a fully genuine relationship with the resurrected Lord, Jesus Christ, Amen."

Into the Inferno

Kuwaiti citizens who awoke early on the morning of February 22, 1991, were greeted by an eerie, horrifying sight. The desert seemed to have erupted. Clouds of fire had sprung from the ground, and dense black smoke banks were eating up the sky. Later, the world would learn that on this day, at dawn, Iraqi military had begun igniting Kuwait's vast oil fields. Almost 90 percent of that country's producing wells were turned into roaring blowtorches. Sixty million barrels of crude oil were going up in smoke each day.

The result was one of the worst man-made ecological disasters of modern times. Aside from the destruction of living things in the firestorm, the smoke from these infernos polluted the air over much of the planet, reaching as far as the Hawaiian Islands. Every war has produced its share of horror and madness. But this act seemed particularly senseless and devastating.

And yet there was something strangely familiar about this apocalyptic landscape. For some, it made vivid certain images that had long rested in the back of their minds. Take the picture portrayed in Revelation 14:10, 11. Speaking of the one who follows and worships the antichrist, John wrote: "He will be tormented with burning sulfur.... And

INTO THE INFERNO 49

the smoke of their torment rises for ever and ever."

A little later in the book of Revelation, when John pictures the burning of wicked Babylon, he uses the same phrase: " 'The smoke from her goes up for ever and ever' " (Revelation 19:3). The burning oil fields of Kuwait have given us a rather stunning preview of earth's final fire. But this raises a very important question: "If Kuwait's inferno was such an intolerable disaster—something no one in his right mind wanted to continue—what about the fires of hell? What about that smoke that ascends forever and ever? Is God's final solution for the wicked to be a ceaseless inferno?"

Let's try to get a clear picture from the Bible of what will happen at the end of time.

Revelation 20 describes Satan's final attempt to overthrow God's government. The Holy City descends from heaven. Satan marshals the legions of the host to attack the city. The righteous saved are securely inside the city with Jesus. Then the Bible says:

> They [the wicked] marched across the breadth of the earth and surrounded the camp of God's people, the city he loves. But fire came down from heaven and devoured them (Revelation 20:9).

There are two key points here. First, the fires of hell originate *in heaven* at the end of the age. According to Hebrews 12:29, our God is a consuming fire. The righteous character of an all-powerful God consumes sin at the end of time.

The second vital point in this passage is that the fire "devours" the wicked. It totally destroys or annihilates them. Would a loving God burn sinners in hell, delighting in their agony for millions and millions of years? Certainly

50 WHEN FAITH CRUMBLES

not! It's at this point that fire comes down from heaven and devours them. The wicked are cast into the lake of fire called "the second death" (verse 14).

Now, it's possible to imagine that there is a lake of fire somewhere out in space. But the clear implication from Scripture is that the lake of fire exists right here on this earth. This is where the final battle is waged; this is where fire from heaven strikes and devours; this is where the dead come forth to judgment. We have no hint of any other place of destruction other than this earth.

But now, let's move on to the next chapter, chapter 21. The first verse tells us that there is to be a new heaven and a new earth; the old earth will pass away. Verse 2 describes a New Jerusalem descending to the earth. John tells us, " 'Now the dwelling of God is with men' " (verse 3). Then we hear a wonderful promise: " 'He [God] will wipe every tear from their eyes [the eyes of the redeemed]. There will be no more death or mourning or crying or pain, for the old order of things has passed away' " (verse 4).

But you'll recall that Revelation 20 described a lake of fire *on the earth*. This presents an enormous problem. If that smoke of torment is still ascending, for ever and ever, there will still be a great deal of mourning and crying and pain. The old order will definitely not have passed away.

To put it simply, you can't have heaven and hell in the same place. Some people question whether you can have hell and heaven in the same universe.

How are we to resolve the conflict? Let's take a closer look at those raging infernos in the Kuwait desert.

The Boots and Coots team of oil-fire specialists were assigned to Number 360, an especially dangerous well. The thunderhead of smoke erupting from it was the size of several football fields. The firefighters circled the well at some distance, trying to get a glimpse of the wellhead. It rumbled like a freight train; they could feel the intense heat

INTO THE INFERNO 51

through the soles of their boots.

The problem was getting close enough to the well to work on it—without becoming incinerated. Fifty thousand gallons of sea water had to be pumped into a nearby pit. Two massive pumps sprayed water on the site at the rate of eight thousand gallons a minute. But this did very little to the wall of flame; it served only to protect the men. Each person had to drink three gallons of ice water during a shift. Otherwise, he could be killed by dehydration from the fiery heat. The firefighters had to wear metal hard hats; the plastic kind would have melted on their heads. Men maneuvering machinery toward the site had to work behind large metal heat shields.

Finally, the crew was able to position a fifty-five-gallon steel drum, loaded with dynamite. They touched off the explosives, creating a huge vacuum. The explosion sucked up oxygen and suffocated the fire. Number 360 had ceased to be an inferno.

These men who braved the oil fires of Kuwait have something to tell us about staring into an inferno. It means one thing—total and complete destruction. They have seen the remains of those who perished in intense fires. There wasn't much left, just a few bone fragments fused to metal.

Now, let me ask you. What is going to happen to those who are thrown into a *lake* of fire? How long will they survive? Isn't it true that the bigger the fire, the quicker the death? To torture someone for a long time, you would need a very small flame—not a great conflagration. Could the Bible be trying to tell us something by calling this lake of fire the second *death*?

But the Bible says "They [the wicked] will be tormented day and night for ever and ever" (Revelation 20:10). How are we to explain that?

Let's look at some other verses in the Bible that shed light on this problem. Hebrews 9:12 states that Jesus obtained "eternal redemption" for us. Hebrews 6:2 speaks of "eternal judgment." Now, we know that Christ's great act of redemption took place at one specific time. And we know that the final judgment takes place at one specific time—it won't go on forever. But still the Bible refers to these as "eternal redemption" and "eternal judgment." Why? Because the *results* of redemption and judgment will be everlasting.

It's the same with "eternal punishment." What is eternal about the fire and the torment? Is it the fire or the consequences of the fire that are eternal? You may find it interesting to discover that there is explicit scriptural teaching for the point of view that it is the *consequences* that are eternal. The end result is eternal death, the second death.

First, let's look at a verse in the very brief book of Jude. The author describes the wickedness of those who lived in Sodom and Gomorrah, and then he says, "They serve as an example of those who suffer the punishment of eternal fire" (Jude 7). There's that phrase again: "eternal fire." But Sodom and Gomorrah aren't still burning. That "eternal fire" went out long ago.

But we have even clearer statements about the fate of the wicked. Listen to the apostle Peter: "The present heavens and earth are reserved for fire, being kept for the day of judgment and destruction of ungodly men" (2 Peter 3:7). For Peter, the fire at the end of the world meant the *destruction* of ungodly men.

The apostle Paul agreed. Concerning those who had become enemies of the cross of Christ, he said, "Their destiny is destruction" (Philippians 3:19). The Greek word Paul used for *destruction* is the strongest word that could be used to mean utter loss of existence.

Please understand this. Throughout the Bible there is one dominant picture of the destiny of the wicked—and that is death. Prophets and apostles united in making the picture forceful. The wicked, they all affirm, will die, perish, be burnt up, utterly consumed, become ashes, become as if they had never existed. Friends, Scripture is clear. The wages of sin is death, not eternal life in hell. It's no good assuming that the body is destroyed in hell but that the soul goes on suffering. Jesus would disagree. He warned of "the one who can destroy both soul and body in hell" (Matthew 10:28). That's plain enough, isn't it?

Of course, to be honest, we must admit that, taken by themselves, those images in Revelation about torment and smoke ascending forever might lend themselves to a picture of a hell that goes on eternally. But we have a basic choice to make as we look at the information the Bible gives us. We can use the Bible's many statements about the death and complete destruction of the wicked to help us understand the vivid images of Revelation. Or we can isolate the vivid images of Revelation—take them out of their context—and develop our own interpretation of Scripture based on these isolated statements, ignoring all the rest that the Bible has to say about the subject.

We have many clear statements in Scripture about the fate of the wicked—they will die, perish, be burnt up, utterly consumed, become ashes, etc. As we've seen, the New Testament consistently uses the word *destruction* to describe their end. In interpreting the Bible, such literal passages should always take precedence over symbolic passages.

I believe the Bible teaches that one day there will be a new world where the horrible traces of sin will linger no longer. Hell and the grave will be gone forever—consumed in the smoke that burns the wicked to ashes. And out of the ashes of the old world God will create a glorious new one.

The passages that describe the smoke of the wicked's torment ascending forever occur in the highly symbolic book of Revelation. This book describes many events that few people take literally. Beasts arising from the sea and a dragon that wages war against a woman are obviously symbols. Revelation is apocalyptic literature, and one of the characteristics of that kind of writing is its use of vivid symbols.

The lake of fire itself is always associated with symbolic creatures—the dragon and the beast are thrown into it. Please don't misunderstand me. Hell is certainly going to be very real. It is not just some psychological state. The Bible describes very real flames at the end of the world. But doesn't it make sense to allow the clear statements of Scripture regarding the death of the wicked to help us see what is ultimately going to happen in that lake of fire?

These vivid images about an eternal fire and the smoke of endless torment are metaphors that emphasize the almost unimaginable tragedy of the lost. Think of it, to be separated from God for ever and ever and ever! To miss out on the eternal joys of the redeemed! To disappear, with no hope of ever existing again! That is a mind-boggling tragedy. And that is what the fiery scenes in Revelation are making vivid for us.

A hell that destroys the wicked forever, not one that keeps them alive forever, is the best way to put together all the biblical evidence. And furthermore, it's the one that reinforces the picture of a loving God, whom Scripture celebrates.

Those raging oil fires in the desert of Kuwait taught us something valuable. To many people, that little spot on the earth may not have seemed very significant. But when the inferno started and the smoke began billowing up, everyone took notice. It affected the environment for thousands of miles around it. We all knew that this ecological disaster had to be stopped. Somehow the fires had to be put out—as quickly as possible.

INTO THE INFERNO 55

I don't believe that those who find a home with God on His new earth will be any less sensitive. No one will be able to rest if ceaseless torment is going on in some corner of God's universe. The fires of hell must be put out; they must be put out whatever the cost.

You know, that's part of the heroism of Christ on the cross. He suffered the second death in our place; He walked into the fires of hell. Christ had to single-handedly cap the spewing well of sin that was destroying humanity. He had to absorb that deadly blaze in His own body. Jesus experienced the agony of hell so that we could live forever with Him. That's the best news of all. Those who place their faith in Christ won't be touched by that final, blazing inferno.

God *does* have a plan for cleansing our universe of sin; completely, irrevocably, eternally, He *will* wipe away every tear and end all suffering.

I'm sure you want to be among those who enjoy the new earth with God and who are not consumed in the old world with Satan. You can make sure you are part of God's great plan as we pray.

* * *

"Dear Father, I thank You so much that You will make a final end to sin and suffering. I also thank You for telling us exactly how we can escape that final inferno. We wholeheartedly accept the rescue that Jesus has created—so heroically. We accept His sacrifice for our guilt. We place our faith in Him as our Saviour. Keep us close to You, until that day when You come to make all things new. In Jesus' name. Amen."

The World of Tomorrow

After fifteen years of searching for the missing pharaoh in the Valley of the Kings, Howard Carter was almost ready to give up his quest. It was 1922.

The archaeologist had invested a good part of his life digging near the monuments and tombs that others had excavated before him. Thirty-three royal tombs had been discovered in the Valley, but all had been plundered by thieves. The experts concluded that this burial ground of pharaohs had yielded all its secrets.

But Howard Carter thought otherwise. He insisted that the tomb of boy king Tutankhamen had to be somewhere in the area. He'd found a cup, pieces of gold foil, and pottery jars—all bearing Tutankhamen's name.

Carter's excavations, however, had come up empty. And his sponsor, Lord Carnarvon, now declared that he could no longer finance the archaeologist's expeditions. Carter desperately pleaded for one last chance. If he didn't find the tomb, he said, he'd pay for the work himself. Lord Carnarvon agreed to give him one more opportunity.

In early November, Carter's workmen uncovered a staircase. The staircase led to a door. Examining it, Carter noticed the seal of the jackal god. "It was a thrilling moment," he wrote later, "for an excavator in that valley of unutterable silence." The jackal seal was affixed to royal tombs. And it had not been broken. Carter cabled his sponsor, asking him to come to the site.

The morning after Lord Carnarvon arrived, Carter cut a hole through the doorway. It was November 7, 1922, the most wonderful day of his whole life. He lifted a candle and peered in. "For a moment," Carter wrote, "I was struck dumb with amazement." He saw "strange animals, statues, and gold—everywhere the glint of gold."

Until that moment, no one had imagined the staggering wealth, the dazzling art, or the royal glory that lay hidden in the sand. Effigies of gods and goddesses, jewels, chests, ivory vases, gilded furniture, and most stunning of all: the sarcophagus of Tutankhamen, a series of beautifully crafted golden statues, each fitting inside the other. They revealed a death mask of beaten gold; finally the world looked on the handsome features of the boy king who ruled only nine years and died under mysterious circumstances in 1350 B.C.

Let's contrast the fate of this boy king Tutankhamen with that of another ruler in Egypt who lived about two hundred years earlier.

During the time that Thutmose I presided on the throne of Egypt, a son was born to two Hebrew slaves, Amram and Jochebed. This was baby Moses, whom Providence and a desperate mother placed in a basket on the River Nile. Princess Hatshepsut found and adopted the child, but let his real Hebrew mother raise him.

For nearly twelve years, Jochebed taught her son to obey and trust the God of heaven; she instilled in Moses a sense of divine calling. Then the boy was taken from his humble home to the royal palace to become, officially, the son of the princess.

Thutmose decided to make this adopted grandson his successor to the throne. He saw to it that the boy was

58 WHEN FAITH CRUMBLES

properly educated for his high position. Moses received the best civil and military training the court of Pharaoh could offer. All steps led him to the glory of Egypt's throne, then the center of the civilized world. All its wealth, influence, and power would lie at his feet, his for the taking—*if* he would just give his allegiance to Aton and Osiris instead of to the God of heaven. Pharaoh's palace would be his home. The Valley of the Kings would provide a final resting place. His body would be entombed with the finest treasures of the land.

But no archaeologist's spade has ever broken through the tomb of King Moses. And no expedition ever will, because no tomb was ever built. Moses made one of history's most critical decisions:

> By faith Moses, when he had grown up, refused to be known as the son of Pharaoh's daughter. He chose to be mistreated along with the people of God rather than to enjoy the pleasures of sin for a short time (Hebrews 11:24, 25).

Moses looked beyond the palaces, beyond the gilded chariots and jeweled vessels and ivory furniture. He didn't want to be buried with such relics. He didn't want to be encased in gold. Moses chose a different fate; he chose to become the son of the mighty King, the God of heaven. He chose to serve Him.

Many years later, Moses died alone on top of Mount Nebo, gazing out at the Promised Land he would never enter. No royal fanfare, no elaborate funeral, no glorious tomb. Had it been a fair exchange? A life of struggle with the wandering children of Israel for the riches and power of Egypt's throne? An apparently insignificant ending for a place in the Valley of the Kings?

To answer that, let's go back to the tomb of Tutankhamen. Why did the Egyptians seal in all these treasures with a dead king?

The answer involves their idea of how to prepare for the afterlife. The ancients believed they could provide the deceased with accessories that would enable them to go on living in the style to which they had become accustomed. They believed the pharaohs had to travel first class in the mysterious journey from life to the world of the dead. That's why Tutankhamen's tomb was stuffed with beautiful furniture, exquisitely carved utensils, elaborate chests, and vessels of oil.

Moses had virtually no power. No one hammered out a gilded death mask for him. But let's discover his ultimate fate. What does the Bible teach regarding the wisdom of Moses' choice?

We gain some remarkable insight in the little book of Jude. Jude 9 suggests that there was a debate between our Lord Himself and Satan after Moses died. There was a dispute regarding resurrecting Moses. Of course, Satan wanted Moses to remain locked in his grave. But the Lord raised Moses bodily from the grave to live forever as a representative of all those who will be resurrected when Jesus comes. Scripture is not describing some disembodied spirit or Moses' immortal soul. Moses was literally, bodily resurrected from the dead, just like we will be when Jesus comes.

Let's move forward in the story centuries later. We go to the top of a certain mountain in Judea: the Mount of Transfiguration. Jesus Christ is transfigured before three of His disciples. His garment becomes a dazzling white; His face seems to shine like the sun. And then two figures, Moses and Elijah, appear with him. Moses, resurrected from the grave, is a representative of those who will be resurrected bodily when Jesus comes. Elijah, who was translated to heaven without seeing death, represents those who will be taken to heaven without seeing death. And there on the Mount of Transfiguration, they're talking with their Friend, Jesus, giving Him encouragement.

This brief scene shows us Moses' remarkable fate. Apparently our heavenly Father just couldn't resist taking Moses to heaven—ahead of time, before that hour when the Bible says all the righteous will be taken up to heaven with Christ at His coming. So what fate did Moses find at the end of his long, hard journey? He found a better Promised Land. He found himself face to face with Jesus Christ, in the Father's house.

Yes, I'd say Moses made a good exchange. I'd rather be talking with Jesus in heaven than lying in a gilded sarcophagus, no matter how many jewels or how much gold surrounds me. I'd rather be walking in my Father's house than lying with the wealth of pharaohs.

Moses saw, by faith, that all the razzle-dazzle in this world is nothing compared to the vastness of God's riches in eternity. He was one of those great men of faith celebrated in the book of Hebrews whose eyes were firmly fixed on "the city with foundations, whose architect and builder is God" (Hebrews 11:10).

The apostle John describes that heavenly city in the book of Revelation. What he saw in vision was so dazzling that he used every metaphor, every shining gem, he could think of, trying to express its glory. He called it "a bride beautifully dressed for her husband" (Revelation 21:2). Its gates, he said, appear to be giant pearls; all its streets are gold. The river of life flows down its center, clear as crystal, bordered by the tree of life bearing a dozen different fruits for "the healing of the nations" (Revelation 22:2).

This is the place Moses looked forward to, a place where every sorrow, every tear, is wiped away. The many beautiful mansions our Father has prepared are for the living, not the dead. The prophet Isaiah pictures a land where the blind see, the lame leap, and the dumb hear. A place where the desert blossoms and the lion and lamb lie down together. It's a place where there's no sickness, no crime, no dying, no getting exhausted at the end of the week (see Isaiah 35:1-10; 65:17-25).

Heaven is not some fairy-tale world—not some world of ethereal, spiritlike beings. Heaven is a real place. God created this earth to be inhabited by healthy, happy, holy beings. According to the Bible, this earth will be recreated in all the splendor of Eden. It will become the perfect home for the saved.

But some have wondered what we would find to do in such a perfect world. Most of our activities here on this earth revolve around dealing with the kinds of problems that don't exist there. Will we just hang around idly strumming our golden harps?

First, we have to get beyond this idea of heaven as some wispy bank of clouds "way beyond the blue." The heavenly city—the New Jerusalem, the cosmic control center of the universe, the nerve center of millions of worlds—will actually become the capital of none other than planet Earth. In Revelation, John saw it "coming down out of heaven from God," to a new and perfect earth where sin no longer exists, "for the first heaven and the first earth had passed away" (Revelation 21:2, 1).

This earth will be completely renewed, returned to its pristine state, a new Eden. It will be a glorious new frontier to explore.

How will we keep busy? The truth of the matter is that in the earth made new we will be free to experience life as it was originally meant to be. So much holds us back now; we waste so much energy in resentment and anxiety and guilt. We go in circles.

But in the new earth, we'll finally be let loose. We'll finally be able to release our creativity and fulfill our dreams. Have you ever gotten caught up in designing your "perfect dream house"? Remember how exciting that can be? You imagined a cozy little study on the second floor or a sparkling swimming pool by the patio. With a shaky economy and the financial pressures of just surviving today, a dream house may seem impossible. You may live in a tenement apartment in one of America's major cities. Home ownership may seem impossible to you.

Isaiah tells us that the new earth will be a place where those "someday" plans become real. Listen: " 'They will build houses and dwell in them; they will plant vineyards and eat their fruit. . . . My chosen ones will long enjoy the work of their hands' " (Isaiah 65:21, 22).

Our hands and our minds were designed by God to build and create and work out our dreams. Immortality isn't immobility. We'll be producing things then that are inconceivable to us now.

But think of another dimension to life in the heavenly city. Think of all the times you've had to say goodbye, all the times you've had to say, "If we only had more time together . . ." One of the greatest joys for people in heaven will be—other people.

There is so much that keeps us apart on earth now and so much that keeps us relating to each other on a superficial level. But in the earth made new, all the barriers come down. We can develop rich and satisfying relationships with an infinite variety of friends.

I'm sure you have people you'd like to see. Perhaps you even have a son or daughter who was taken from you. And you can't wait to throw your arms around them again. Friends, heaven is about reunion. It's about getting together in ways we never have before. It's about wonderful, stimulating relationships.

And the greatest, most exciting reunion of all will be the day we walk up to Jesus Christ and see Him at last face to

THE WORLD OF TOMORROW 63

face! In the new earth, we'll be able to talk with the One whose presence is so brilliant it makes the Sun seem unnecessary. We'll be able to unite our voices in a chorus of ecstatic praise—that's almost too much to think about. But the apostle Paul did give it some thought. During a time of persecution, he told the Corinthians in a passionate declaration, "Our light and momentary troubles are achieving for us an eternal glory that far outweighs them all" (2 Corinthians 4:17). Eternal glory for Paul meant the glory of being with Jesus.

That's what Moses chose, and it did indeed outweigh everything else. It outweighed all the gold and silver and gems that could be stuffed into the largest tomb in the Valley of the Kings. Moses came to talk with Jesus on the Mount of Transfiguration. He came to talk with an old Friend. That was better than anything the palaces of Egypt could offer. I have imagined myself meeting Jesus in heaven. Gently He places His nail-scarred hand upon my shoulder. All the reminders of sin are gone except one—the nail prints in His hands. His compassionate, understanding eyes reveal that He knows everything about me yet loves me still. The One who knows me best loves me most. In words of tenderest compassion, He gently inquires, "Can we spend some time together?" My heart beats with eager anticipation. The Creator of the universe, the Redeemer of the world wants to spend time with me!

As we begin walking down a grassy, tree-lined lane, crossing a clear, babbling brook, Jesus kindly says, "Bend over; drink some of this life-giving water." The water of the river of life flowing from the throne of God is invigorating; it's life-giving. He leads me to the tree of life, placing its fruit directly in my hands. As I eat it my whole body tingles with the sensation of health. I have never felt so good before.

He stretches out His nail-scarred hands, gently saying, "If you ever begin to doubt My love, remember these." All I can do is fall at His feet and worship Him.

How can you possibly turn your back on One who loves you so much? How can you possibly walk away from Him? He longs to take a walk with you in eternity. He longs to reveal the mysteries of His love. He longs to hold you in His arms, safe and secure forever. This is no dream. It's no make-believe tale. It's reality today—right now. This moment I invite you into the security of His love forever.

Imagine what it will be like to see heaven itself, Jesus Christ Himself, descend to this planet at His second coming! I want to be a part of the great reunion. I want my life aimed toward that eternal glory that outweighs all of my present difficulties. I want to put my life in the hands of Jesus Christ the Saviour today, so I can see Him face to face tomorrow.

Isn't that the deepest desire in your heart as well? Let's determine to be ready for that wonderful reunion now, as we pray.

* * *

"Dear Father, thank You for giving us glimpses of heaven. Thank You that our destiny can be far more than gold accessories in a silent tomb. We want to be among those who live life to the fullest—in the New Jerusalem. We want to be among those who unite in thrilling praise of our old Friend, Jesus Christ. So we commit our lives to Him now as our Lord and Saviour. Keep us close; keep us faithful. In His name. Amen."